Signposts of Dying

First Printing, 2016

ISBN 978-0-9971165-1-9

Martha Jo Atkins, LLC
PO Box 700212
San Antonio, Texas 78270-0212

www.MarthaAtkins.com

Praise for Signposts of Dying: What You Need to Know

Good things come in small packages. This is particularly the case with Signposts by Martha Jo Atkins. This simple and beautifully written book covers great territory. Atkins shares with readers the common signposts of the dying process—and does so tenderly and truthfully. Signposts speaks of our shared inevitability and the universal processes that mark our path as we leave this world behind. Easy to read, filled with great information and penned with love, Signposts is a book that every human being should own. Each of us will, sooner or later, be called to stand at the threshold with someone we care for. Knowing the signposts will help us all move more gracefully across the portal.

—Lisa Smartt, Founder
The Final Words Project

So very, very moving, and helpful, and real. A lot resonates with what I have heard others report. Some I thought was familiar, but then the way it was presented made me pause, then stop, then really absorb it in a fresh way. Some was brand new. What a gift this is! Thank you!

—Jan Dawson

This book is a TREASURE. I'm a big old puddle of tears ... it's like having you right here speaking to me ... walking me through it. I can see this sweet book of comfort and truth being passed from friend to friend ... from generation to generation.

—Sarah Seidelmann

What a gift you have given to this world through your book! It took me back to both of the times that I've had the privilege to support and bear witness to two dear friends' passings. I wish I had known that everything foreign feeling that I was witnessing were the perfectly normal signposts of the dying process. The book is well written, concise, and a wealth of information. Thank you!

—Kathryn McCormick

What a gift this will be to those who are dying and who are sitting alongside them.

—Steph Marks-Ryan

Reading this book is like seeing the sun peeking over the horizon and knowing that pretty soon it will be shining on so many people, warming them and lighting their way. I am so happy for you and so happy for all the people who will be helped by this.

—Jean Dallas

This book will be a gift to all who read it. Its greatest contribution is the richness with which it affirms the experiences of both the dying and those who will be left behind. The love you bring to this subject is abundantly clear. But love without wisdom is useless, and your wisdom shines through like a beacon of light for all who are experiencing one of the most difficult times of their lives.

—Liz Parker

What a deep pleasure to read this so profound, so much needed in the world, so lovingly written book! I so like how you invite the reader to change perspective. To see the dying person as someone who gets ready for a journey ... an experience we all share. I like the clarity of the structure and how everything is so well explained and underlined with examples. I love your friendly and reassuring tone which makes it easy to connect and which surely helps to ease the fear which often goes with dying. What a great gift and touching book! So helpful to get death and dying out of the taboo zone in a heartwarming way which allows everyone to have and express their feelings. And at the same time to give space for the needs of the dying person and to understand them more.

—Nina Riede

Signposts of Dying:
What You Need to Know

MARTHA JO ATKINS, PHD

For Noble – as a wee one you guided me to love language and as an adult you've helped me see my work anew. I thank you.

About the Author

Dr. Martha Jo Atkins teaches about death, dying, and grief. Dr. Atkins provides on-demand courses, coaching, and other tools to help you meaningfully navigate the tricksy transitional parts of life.

Prior to owning her own training and consulting company, Dr. Atkins founded the Children's Bereavement Center of South Texas (www.cbcst.org) where she served as executive director for eight years.

Dr. Atkins' Ph.D. studies, and now her continuing research, focus on the trajectory of dying and how deathbed phenomena affect the dying person and those who love them.

Her first book *Signposts of Dying* was published in 2016. Dr. Atkins' training and research institute also opened in 2016.

Dr. Atkins lives in south Texas with her partner Suzette. Critical fact: Dr. Atkins' favorite drink is an ice cold Dr. Pepper.

sign post

ˈsīnˌpōst/

noun

• A sign giving information, such as the direction and distance to a nearby town, typically found at a crossroads.

• Something that acts as guidance or a clue to an unclear or complicated issue.

(From Google, 2015)

CONTENTS

Foreword

When my friend Nina was dying of ALS, one day a nurse whispered to me, "She is now actively dying."

"Aren't we all?" I responded, a bit stunned by her statement.

Aren't we all.

There is a core truth about the human condition: It ends. This is a truth that none of us escape, however desperately we may try. We die. Someone watches us die. We sit vigil while others die while we watch, or we flee in those moments.

Why do we often flee? Because death is unknown, frightening, and so much bigger than we are; it is fearful until we have experienced the honor and gift of being a witness to final moments—until we *know*.

Fear stems from ignorance. And what is the antidote to ignorance? Learning.

My friend Howard has quadriplegia as the result of an accident decades ago now. I remember him first telling me about how scared people are around him. "Why?" I asked innocently. "Because," he said, "they're thinking 'there but for the grace of God go I' and they can't stand that reminder of their own vulnerability."

And so it is with death. We flee, in part, because each

death reminds us of our own end. For this moment we can think to ourselves, 'there but for the grace of God go I' ... but this moment is fleeting, and we know that.

In this book, Martha Jo Atkins has taken us gently and firmly to this place, this moment, this apex of great fear and pain, and she has said, with all the tenderness in the world, "Look."

This is a book that provides us a roadmap of a journey that will be personal and unique for each of us— whether in our own dying or in staying the course as a witness to the dying process of another. This is a book that will allow us to stay near the fire with someone as they go. You will recognize yourself in these pages, and also be surprised. As a result of reading this book, you will be prepared for the process when you are called to be a part of it, as I was:

> The nurses knew things I could never know, about how her body was shutting down. I thought she would survive. Surely she would. For five hours that night, Nina was alive again, strong and ferocious and manic. Struggling to tell me something, her arms stretched straight up into the sky toward the ceiling pockmarked with tiny holes, her eyes so wide, looking past me and through me. She was wailing and looking up, like a pilgrim who has had a vision. I got used to it. It stopped scaring me. "Nina," I whispered, leaning down to her ear, "I feel like I'm failing you at this important moment. I

know you are trying to tell me something, and I don't know what." She moved her arms to her heart, over and over again. Suddenly, without any warning, she opened her arms again and grabbed me toward her, pulling me up and over the bed rails with a strength long since gone from her arms, but now back. She held me the tightest I have ever been held, my torso on top of hers, the bottom half of my body dangling over the metal rail. She held me.

This book provides clear signposts for journeys such as that one with Nina. I didn't know and was fearful, and now I do, thanks to Martha Atkins' work. Now I know that naming the signposts can free us to be fully present for the miracles inherent in those moments of those last, important journeys.

Patti Digh
Author of *The Geography of Loss: Embrace What Is, Honor What Was, Love What Will Be*

Introduction

I watched my mother watching something under her closed eyelids. "Mom, what do you see?"

She lay in the hospital bed in the living room of her home. I held her hand atop a beautiful multi-colored quilt her friends had made for her.

"Daddy Charlie and Grandmother. Mother and Daddy. Uncle Claude and Aunt Lala."

"Where are they?" I asked.

"Walking up the road from the farmhouse."

I imagined my great-grandparents, grandparents, uncle and aunt walking side by side toward my mother. In these moments Mom was calm and peaceful after several days of having not been either of those.

I was curious. My brother Jim had died years before. I imagined when the time came for family to be nearby to help my mother cross from this world, Jim would be there.

I'd had a dream Jim was sitting in a chair, reading a book, waiting for Mom to be ready to go. I remember calling my brother, John, and sharing my dream. He'd had a similar one. We marveled at the coincidence.

Back in the room with my mother, I had to ask, "Mom,

1

where's Jim?"

Eyes still closed and with a slightly bigger smile she said, "Oh, he's been here."

I don't know if she meant been and left or if she meant he's been here a long time waiting for me. Either way I was comforted.

That experience with Mom opened up a deep curiosity in me about the dying process. I've done some kind of death, dying, and grief work since I was 21 but there had never been deep or enduring conversations about this part – the visits, the non-ordinary experiences that happen around dying.

My dissertation research included the sights, sounds, language and behaviors of the dying as witnessed by those at the bedside. Since 2005 I've studied, pondered, and heard many stories about deathbed phenomena. I regularly get calls or emails from people who are with a dying person and have questions about the process. This book is an explanation of the way I see dying now. I say *now* because I'm still learning.

This is a guidebook about dying – a resource to help you understand some of what you may see, hear, and experience when you are with someone who is taking leave of this world. This is not an exhaustive explanation, rather something you can pick up and use to find answers when the terrain is unfamiliar.

Specifically this guidebook is for people caring for someone on hospice, someone who is dying, or someone who may be on hospice soon. Hospice provides professional care, medication, emotional, and spiritual support for the dying and for those who love them. Go to www.caringinfo.org to learn more about hospice.

Caveat: Some people who are sick, not dying, engage in a few of the experiences I'll be describing.

If your person is *not* on hospice, please do not assume they are dying now or soon because they're demonstrating some of these behaviors. For instance, often people diagnosed with dementia, or elderly patients who have a fever, may have visions or dreams of people they don't know or people they know who have died.

There are many factors involved in determining if someone is dying. If you're concerned about someone you love and your person is not under the care of hospice, your healthcare professional is the point of contact for questions you may have.

Why This Book?

There are recognizable, identifiable signposts in the dying process, a trajectory of experiences I want to teach you. Here's why:

- If you understand the signposts, my hope is they won't frighten you when you see them or hear them, nor will you dismiss them as nonsense. You'll have context.

- Context can help when the waiting gets long as it's wont to do when your lover or your child or parent is dying.

- Context can help when your person begins doing or saying things they've never done or said before. You'll know your beloved isn't crazy, nor are you.

- Context can help when your person needs reassurance. You'll know what's happening and can offer comfort. You can meet them where they are.

I gave a San Antonio TEDx talk in 2013, "More to Dying Than Meets the Eye". (Here is the link to my TEDx talk www.marthaatkins.com/TEDx2013). I began to receive emails. Some were from family members who had questions. Others expressed gratitude for helping them understand what was happening as they sat at their beloved's bedside. I wasn't expecting that.

Then there were emails that started like this:

"I'm 35 years old and dying."

"I'm a 49-year-old metastatic breast cancer patient with mets to my liver."

"I don't know how long I have, and I don't want to spend whatever time I have left dying and in fear. I'm trying to instill in my family not to be afraid because I know there is more...I have sent this beautiful [TEDx] video to my children, closest family, and friends..."

"I watched your TEDx video, and a lot of it is kinda what I am experiencing even now. My dreams are becoming more vivid...it's like the next step or phase is getting closer..."

I was, and still am, so glad to get notes like these. If you ever see me teared up at my desk, I'm likely reading a tender email.

Professionally, things were perking along. Then in the Spring of 2014, my father got sick. My personal and professional worlds collided.

I sat at my papa's bedside, as a daughter and a researcher, watching him engage in the behaviors and speak the language I'd learned about over the previous

5

nine years. I was in awe and heartbroken, certain he was leaving us. It was an extraordinary time — he didn't die.

I rolled the experiences we had with Papa over and over in my head. I'd think about stories I'd heard from clients and strangers. I thought about my family members' deaths. I read and re-read a note my Aunt Betty left on her table. I began to see patterns in movements and language. What I'd seen before as random, I now saw on a trajectory.

I've been thinking about writing for the last two years. Thank you for reading. I'm honored to share what I've learned with you and I hope what you take away will somehow ease your journey.

The Dying Process: Predictable And Not

The dying process is as individual as a snowflake or a thumbprint and also somewhat predictable. The similarities are in movement, language, and behaviors. Not every dying person demonstrates all the things we'll talk about in this guidebook. That's part of the individuality of the experience.

Some who are dying have a prolonged experience. Some, shorter. Some people, it seems, have an easier dying experience. Some are more awake and able to communicate until the very end. Some not. If you have been at the bedside of someone who was dying, the next death you attend will likely be different. And the next death after that, different still.

As oxymoronic as it may seem, there is predictability in the behaviors and language of the dying. Words and movements that seem to change as the dying person nears death are common across cultures around the world. I call these *signposts*, clues that can help you understand more about what's happening in your beloved's world as they work toward leaving their body.

Caveat: Signposts are NOT predictors of imminent death nor are they prescriptive of a specific timeline.

Example: If your dying friend is telling you about seeing her favorite Aunt Tilly, who died 20 years ago, the vision of Aunt Tilly does not necessarily mean your friend is going to die in the next hour. It does mean your friend has taken another step on the trajectory of the dying process. (Keep reading! I'll talk more about this later.)

Remember:

• The signposts are not prescriptive.

• They likely will not happen in the exact order in which they're written in this guidebook.

• Your person may not experience all of the signposts outlined. Sometimes they can't because they're medicated. Sometimes their cues are so subtle we miss them.

• Awareness of the signposts will not give you superpowers to know the hour your person will die.

• Awareness of the signposts will give you context and hopefully ease some of the anxiety that comes with unpredictability.

Signpost: Saying Good-bye

Think about times in your life when you've had to tell someone you love good-bye. Maybe you've moved to the other side of the country. Maybe *the one* turned out not to be.

Or maybe you've had to say good-bye to food you love.

Or your ability to drive a car.

Your ability to care for yourself the way you did in the past.

Your ability to read.

The dying are engaged in a good-bye process.

When my brother Jim died years ago, his death was sudden and unexpected. A couple of his friends went looking when he didn't show up for work. He'd fallen asleep in his bed at home. His big heart had stopped in the night.

Our family began a meaning-making process, thinking about where he'd been and who he'd been with, examining his behaviors over the last year.

His will was complete.

Insurance policies were purchased.

There had been an epic hiking trip with his brother and good friends.

He'd attended a retirement ceremony for my parents.

He'd instigated an impromptu trip to Washington DC with his favorite Aunt Betty.

In retrospect, we saw Jim finishing things. Like a bow on a package. It was comforting, too, noticing how he'd taken care of business. Dying people do that. It's a way to say good-bye.

Your beloved may have stories to tell. They may have drawers they want to clean out. They may have people to call or people for you to call on their behalf. They may wish to hear music from their high school years or to teach you how to make their favorite pie.

These acts and others are all part of saying good-bye to this world and the people in it that they love.

Let them.

You may be inclined to say, "Oh, don't talk that way." Or "We can talk about that later."

If they're opening their heart to you, I invite you to allow yourself to receive what they have to share.

Signpost: Your Beloved Wants To Stop Treatment

In my experience, and much to the chagrin of those around him or her, the person who is sick is often the one who raises the flag to stop treatment and change the course. Sometimes it's a subtle *I'm so tired* and sometimes the words come across like a flashing neon billboard *I'm done. Let's go home.*

For those who love this person and are so deeply invested in keeping them alive, that kind of news is tough to hear.

"No, please. Keep going. Keep fighting. You can do this."

"Don't stop now. God can still heal you."

Duane wrote me, "I want to stop treatment but my family…they want me to keep going. I'm so tired."

If your beloved son or daughter, mother or father, partner, or friend of a lifetime hands you this book and has this particular page marked for you to read, you have an opportunity, an invitation – not an easy one, not one that will make you warm and fuzzy inside, but one that calls you to do something you're going to hear me repeat over and over in the coming pages:

Meet Them Where They Are.

In that place of, this is so unbelievably difficult for all of us.

In that place of, I don't want to live like this anymore.

In that place of, help me do this on my own terms.

In that place of, trust that I know what I need and what

I need doesn't mean I love you any less.

Maya Angelou said, "When someone shows you who they are, believe them the first time." When I talk with dying or grieving people, I trust they are speaking their truth. I believe them when they tell me what they want and need.

Honoring what your beloved wants is simple, but my goodness, it's often not easy.

Signpost: I'm Not Hungry

There are different kinds of *I'm-not-hungry*.

There's the kind that lasts for a day or two, or the one that occurs because it's too tough to swallow.

There's the kind that comes because food doesn't taste the same anymore.

Then there's the *I'm-not-hungry* that happens because your beloved's body is changing its energy cycles. The energy to consume and digest food is being replaced with the energy of dying. Let me say that again. The energy involved to consume and digest food is being replaced with the energy of dying. There is a process of release happening deep in the cells of your beloved. One aspect of that release is the cessation of eating.

But wait: Food is love! Food is life! People gotta eat!

Not when someone is dying.

I wonder if you've heard yourself or someone else say one of these phrases to a hospice patient:

"Come on, Dad, just a bite."

"You're not eating? Come on, you need to eat a little."

"He had hallucinations the last time he didn't eat. We're pushing Ensure."

"His blood sugar will get low. He has to eat something."

An invitation: Believe your beloved. If they don't wish to eat, don't push it. Offer, sure. Cajole, bribe, get mad? There's no need. You're not failing them by not feeding them. True story.

If you find yourself feeling aggravated or sad because your beloved isn't eating, gently I say to you: Feel your feelings. They are valid and important. This not eating business is part of the whole big dying process, and that means someone you love won't be here. If you keep pushing food, that won't keep them here longer.

Encouraging eating or fixing meals is a way for you to do something, to control a piece of an uncontrollable situation. That works right up until the point when your person is finished with that part of their life. Gently I say to you: It's okay.

I surely have been the pusher of food. Once I understood the dying process, I felt guilty. I was trying to help but could've done so differently.

Another great lesson from Maya Angelou, "Do the best you can until you know better. When you know better, do better."

Signpost: Difficulty Swallowing

Your beloved may begin to experience difficulty swallowing. You may see this in conjunction with their not wanting to eat. They may cough when they eat. They may need food mashed up for them.

Just because it was easy for your person to swallow pills yesterday doesn't mean it's easy for them today.

If they say they're having trouble swallowing, or they don't want to take pills any longer, believe them. Yes — when they don't take their pills any longer, things will change. Things are gonna change anyway. This is part of the process.

Sometimes dying people want to taste foods even though they can't swallow them. There's a Sally Field movie that shows this beautifully. Ms. Field's character, who is dying, sits at the kitchen table with her family, chewing her beloved food and spitting it out. Her family is a bit shocked at first, and then a family member joins her, chewing and spitting. Then everyone else joins in with Ms. Field's character leading the way.

Caveat: Sometimes dying people rally.

A rally means the dying person moves from being mostly unresponsive or 'confused' (they're really not) to being present and connected to those in the room around them. It's not uncommon for dying people to ask for food at that time, even though they've not eaten in awhile, even if they have difficulty swallowing. Let 'em taste. Let 'em chew. Just like Ms. Field's character, they don't have to swallow the food.

Signpost: Longing For The Journey

The dying often speak in metaphors and symbolic language. If you listen for that language, you may get clues about your beloved's dying process.

As your beloved talks to you, they may talk about wanting to take a trip. To go somewhere. To ride in a car. The predominant feeling is a longing to go to some other place than where they are now.

They may talk of going home. Leaving. Going. Getting out of here. That other place will become an integral piece of their experience in the coming days. Listen closely and you may be able to hear them process the experience aloud in metaphor as they make their way.

Signpost: I Want To Go Home

When you hear your beloved say *I want to go home*, this can be confusing. Your beloved may be home already, or they may not live at their own home. They may speak of a home they lived in years and years ago.

What in the world is happening?

For those who are dying, journey metaphors are common across the world. Fear not. When this kind of conversation begins, it's not crazy talk. It's a signpost.

If you hear your beloved say *I want to go home*, that does not mean they're going to drop dead tomorrow. I **do** want you to understand that something's up. Some kind of change has happened.

It's common for the dying to speak in the present time of a home they lived in years ago, as though they've been there recently or they live in that place now. They may be confused about where they are, not recognizing the everyday things that are their own. For instance, they may look around the home they've lived in for thirty years and although their things seem familiar, they aren't sure where they are and don't understand the things around them are their own.

It's easy to dismiss this language around going home. I invite you not to.

Minimizing or discounting their experience, trying to

convince them – *You ARE home* – can be crazy-making for both of you. If you discount your beloved's comments, this can be especially frustrating for them.

What can you do? Meet them where they are:

"Mom, I'm confused. I wonder where you think we are?"

"We are at your home, Dad. I wonder what home you're thinking about now?"

You can also reassure your beloved. You could say:

"You're ready to get out of here, aren't you."

"We'll get you home as soon as we can."

"You'll be home soon."

"We'll help you get home, Mom. It's okay for you to rest."

I heard somebody say recently, "Perhaps they are not confused at all; instead it is us." The more I study and learn about dying, I believe that's true.

Signpost: Preparing For The Journey

Think for a moment about what you do to prepare for a trip. What do you gather as you're readying yourself? Your person may begin to talk about gathering things they need for a trip. Even though they're in bed, even though they haven't walked in awhile, even though there's no way they're physically going anywhere, they are focused on readying themselves for a trip.

You may hear your beloved talk about a gathering they need to get to. They need to get to the old gym. Or the car dealership. Or the ranch. These are metaphors. They're leaving their body soon and something inside of them is preparing. The need to get ready, to pull supplies together for the trip, is real for them.

For example, they may ask for their suitcase or bags. They may not be able to tell you why they need those things, but the need is urgent. You may sense their frustration. You may see them trying to get up and out of bed – even if they haven't been out of bed in a long time.

Common Comments:
"I need my suitcase."
"I need my shoes."
"Where is the map? I need the map."
"Would you get my pens for me? And my book. I need my book."
"I need my tools."

How can you respond? Meet them where they are.

Not Helpful:
"You don't need your suitcase, Dad. We're at the hospital. We're not leaving."

Helpful:
"Sure, we'll get your suitcases for you."
"Dad, we've got those for you in the other room."
"It's not quite time to go yet."
"We'll get them when it's time."
"Your suitcase is in a safe place."

Not Helpful:
"You don't need your shoes, Dad. We're at the hospital. We're not leaving."

Helpful:
"Your shoes are right here, Dad. Let's leave them off for just a little bit until they tell us we can go. It's not quite time."

Not Helpful:
"You don't need a map, Mom. We're not going anywhere."

Helpful:
"Mom, the map is in the car, I can get it for you a little later."
"Maybe I can help, Mom. Tell me where you want to go?"

Not Helpful:
"You don't need those things, Dad. You have an IV in your hand. You can't write."

Helpful:
(If you've got them, give them!)
"Dad, here's one of your books and here are your pens. I'll put them right here beside you."
"I don't have yours, but I've got some here you can use anytime. I'll put them right here on your table."

I've seen over and over, once the person has been reassured or their need met, they relax. Their facial expression changes. They may physically lie back in the bed. The whole conversation may begin again a short while later or even the next day. Go with it. This is all part of the magnificent process your beloved must engage in to get them to the next place in the trajectory of dying.

Signpost: Clean It, Move It, Give It Away

Your beloved may be intent on giving things away. Small things. Big things. They need to get a drawer cleaned out. They need to find some papers and get those to Uncle Frank's house. They need to have one more look at those financials.

This may be all your person can talk or think about for a few days.

This is a signpost.

Your beloved is not trying to make you crazy though it may feel a little like that.

Consider that an internal process is happening for them. They're sorting, releasing, opening to new possibilities. The outward experience — figuring things out, making sure everything is as okay as it can be — matches the inner process where I believe the same thing is happening. Sorting is happening. Putting things in their place is happening. Saying good-bye is happening. Once the business is done, they can go.

This sorting process can go on for several months or just a few days. Often I talk with families who are able to recognize the sorting in retrospect. They think back on the weeks and months of their beloved's illness and discover clues. Some people find this helpful to know as it can demonstrate a larger process that has been going on for awhile. The seemingly short illness and sudden death may not be so short or sudden.

Receiving is a tough thing for some of us to do. It is surely difficult to receive as a dying person, as so much autonomy is chipped away bit by bit. I watched a beautiful video of Elisabeth Kübler-Ross speaking to a woman who was dying. The woman wanted to get up and clean. She wanted to do things in her home rather than have them done for her. Such a task to flip from being the person who gives to being the person who receives. Sometimes we see that as a way to lose power. I think it's quite the contrary. Receiving with genuine love and affection is extraordinarily powerful.

If your beloved has things they want to give you, words they need to say, I invite you to practice receiving. This act, this energy exchange between the two of you, will help your beloved with the ongoing internal and external sorting that is part of their dying process.

Signpost: Storytelling

Your beloved has lived a life. There are stories to share. You may experience your person in a full-on *I need to share all the stories I can think of with you.* If you're keen to remember what they share, hit the record button on your phone.

If YOU have things you want to know about from your beloved, now is the time to ask. And now is the time for you to say what you need and want to say.

Circumstances can change in an instant. Your talkative father can lie down for a nap and not awaken. If ever there was a time not to delay conversations, it is now. I get that sometimes we need to build up our courage to share vulnerable aspects of life. Do it. 20 seconds of courage. That's all you need to get started.

Not Helpful:
Waiting until the right time to say what you need to say. Waiting until the right time to allow space for your person to say what they need to say.

Helpful:
"Mom, tell me some more about _____."
"Walter, I want to tell you something. It'll just take a minute."

20 seconds of courage.

Go.

Signpost: Seeing, Hearing And Feeling What You And I Cannot

"Any woman of the people will tell you that when a sick man talks with his own dead folks, there is no longer any hope of his recovery."
Ernesto Bozzano, Apparitions of Deceased Persons at Death-beds The Annals of Psychical Science, Feb. 1906

For at least 600 years, anecdotal accounts have detailed the sights, sounds, and tactile experiences of the dying. These experiences are most often recorded as positive ones bringing comfort to the dying person.

As your beloved moves along the trajectory of dying, he or she may see visions of relatives, unknown persons, animals, religious figures, landscapes, or other things you cannot see.

You may see your person looking around the room or seemingly looking through you.

You may notice them talking to someone you cannot see, holding hands with someone, or reaching out as though engaged in an activity with others in the room.

These experiences have been reported all over the world, in all cultures, from people of all ages, with no regard for religion, education, or socio-economic background. They occur to those who are blind and those who are deaf.

If you are with your beloved and they begin to behave as though others are in the room, they're not crazy. Neither are you.

These experiences are another aspect of the dying process.

Hallucinations or Visions?

There are researchers who are convinced the sights and sounds dying people experience are auditory and visual hallucinations. The cause? Lack of oxygen to the brain. Disease process. Stored memories in the brain releasing themselves.

For each of these scenarios, examples can be given to refute them. I read about a physician whose patient had cancer all over her brain. She also had visions as part of her dying process. The physician was perplexed because the part of the woman's brain needed to function for visions to occur was decimated by cancer.

On the other side of the conversation are those who believe there is a difference between hallucinations and visions, and that the dying indeed are having an experience we can't yet, and maybe won't be able to, explain scientifically.

Hallucinations are different from visions. Hallucinations are often of unfamiliar animals or people, insects, or things moving on the walls. Visitors (those you and I can't see but the dying can) may be critical of the person dying and not friendly. Hallucinations are annoying, sometimes frightening, and easily managed by medication changes.

In contrast, visions your beloved may see include people both known and unknown, known and unknown animals, or religious figures. Your person may hear music "but not like any music I've heard before" or landscapes that are so beautiful they're difficult to describe. Steve Jobs' reported last words: "Oh wow oh wow oh wow." I wonder what he saw!

Visions have been documented when the person is fully lucid and psychologically healthy. One interesting piece from the research is that dying people will speak to the figures they see with complete sentences, which is contrary to hallucinatory experiences. Often the visions are reported as calming and helpful. In some instances, this is not the case though most anecdotal research reports positive experiences.

Hearing the voice of departed loves and seeing them are both commonplace, non-threatening experiences outside Western culture. You may find your beloved is hesitant to say aloud what they're seeing or hearing. They don't want anyone to think they're crazy.

Signpost: Watching Around The Room – Eye Level, Up, Top Of Room, Not Seeing You

It's a little weird at first when your beloved begins looking at things beside you or even looking through you.

There may be movements — waving their arms or hands, or trying to get out of bed — associated with whatever they're seeing.

Later, you may see your beloved watching something under their closed eyelids, their facial expressions changing with what they see.

They may not talk about what they see unless you ask.

I've noticed the places the dying watch in the room change as they move through the dying process, from near them, as though someone is standing beside them, to up midway around the room. Gazing at the ceiling or a corner of the room is also common.

Not Helpful:
"I don't know what you're looking at, Dad."
"Nothing is there."
Saying in front of the dying person, "Don't worry about him, he's out of it."

Helpful:
Sit quietly with them.
Say aloud, "I see you watching something. Tell me

about it."

"Mark, it seems like you're looking at something. What do you see?"

Signpost: Hearing People Talking To Them

It's common for the dying to hear friends or family members calling to them. You may see your person turn their head toward the sound.

I heard and read about that. Then I got to witness it.

In my father's hospital room, I sat by his bed. He turned his head toward me and said, "Mother?" then looked at me quizzically, "Did you hear my mother? Mimi? My mother's calling me." He was so sure of it. I told him I didn't hear her, but I believed him when he said he did.

My dad heard people in the hallway the rest of us couldn't hear.

Not Helpful:
"Dad, just ignore that."
"Nobody's there!"
"You're just hearing things, Gert. Go back to sleep."

Helpful:
"I didn't hear her, Dad. Did she sound far away or close by?"
I did ask my dad that, and he said, "She sounded kind of far away."
Another helpful response could be: "You heard your mom. How about that! Tell me more."

I Invite You To:
Reassure your beloved that it's okay to talk about what's happening with them.

Ask questions.

See if you can get a little bit of conversation started.

You might be able to, you might not, but it helps them know it's okay for them to say those things out loud.

Signpost: Unknown Visitors

Your beloved may see people who are unknown to them. Here's an example:

A gentleman was working on a Sudoku puzzle one afternoon. He'd had cancer for many years.

His wife said, "Dan, sometimes people see things others can't see when they are dying, and I just wondered if you'd ever seen anybody or anything?"

"Yeah. There's a guy that comes and stands by my bed at night."

"What does he look like?"

"He's a soldier. It's a guy dressed like a soldier, like from the – I don't know – 1940s…1930s."

"Does he scare you?"

"No. Not at all."

"Is it your dad?" The man's father had been in the military.

"No, I don't know him."

"Do you see anything else?"

"Yeah. There's a dog that comes and curls up by my

feet, sometimes." He went on to describe the dog. His wife said they decided the dog was one they had early in their relationship of many years.

Notice how the woman needed to ask questions. Her husband wasn't forthcoming. There's a reason for that. The people experiencing the visions don't want to be seen as unstable or crazy. I witnessed that with my dad. He was seeing things around the room and hesitant to share. I perceived him to be more open about what he was seeing when he discovered we wouldn't judge him.

Not Helpful:
"There's no one here."
"You're just seeing things."
"Go back to sleep."

Helpful:
"What are you seeing, Dad?"
"It's unusual isn't it, to see things you can't quite explain."
"You're okay. I'll sit right here with you".
"If what you're seeing is too uncomfortable for you, I can ask for some medicine to help."

Signpost: Known Visitors

Deceased relatives and friends are visitors to dying people. I sometimes refer to these as *Unseens* as they are unseen to us, not to the dying person. These relatives may show up beside the bed, in the corner of the room, or they may walk by in the hallway.

As the trajectory of dying progresses, the visitors may be higher up in the room. Your person's gaze may move from horizontal, as though they're looking at someone standing beside their bed, to up midway around the walls of the room, then up to the ceiling.

There are times when your beloved may look as though they're staring *through* you. They are.

The dying are here, physically present in the moment, and they are also away, off in another place that they have difficulty explaining. Ineffable. If you're talking to your mother and it takes a moment for her to rouse from a staring gaze, that's a hint that she's been in the other place for a bit.

You may notice your person spends more and more time 'away'. This is part of the process.

Not Helpful:
"There's nothing up there, Mom. Look at me, I'm talking to you."
"There's no window over there. We can't open it."

[Saying aloud] "Man, he's staring around the room a lot. What's wrong with him?"

(The dying can hear you and often understand, even when it may not seem so. I invite you to speak in front of them as though they understand it all.)

Helpful:

"Looks like you're watching lots of things around the room. I'd love to hear about who or what you're seeing."

"What do you see, Mom?"

"Are you seeing anyone? Is it Aunt Jan? Or Paul?"

"I know people who are nearing the end of their lives see things the rest of us can't. You're okay. I'm right here with you."

Signpost: Friends Or Guides Who Appear When Family Cannot

Who are the dying seeing? What was clear in my initial research is that companionship from Unseens is personalized, meeting the needs of the dying person in the moment.

Friends and family members are common sights, and unknown friendlies – helpful people or guides – come too.

What about situations where the people in the family of origin were abusive? If your person had a difficult relationship with family members and is worried those people are going to show up, share this next part with them.

A woman told me her husband (I'll call him David) was afraid to die because he didn't want to see his family. David understood about visions of the dying and had no desire to connect with his abusive family. He'd ceased contact long ago.

A few weeks before David died, his wife saw him talking animatedly to someone she couldn't see. Her husband happily introduced her to a young boy about 8 years old. Her husband said the boy had shown up and they'd been playing together.

Unsure what to do at first, David's wife decided "to go with it." She told me her husband was calmer and happier after the arrival of the young boy, who stayed around through the rest of the man's dying process. The abusive relatives never appeared.

As I've shared this story, I've heard similar ones of unknown friendlies appearing to help with the transition.

Not Helpful:
"There's no one here."
"You need some medicine."
"What in the world are you talking about?"

Helpful:
"Nice to meet you, young man."
"I'm glad you're here to help David."
"I'm glad he's here to help you."
"How wonderful."

Signpost: Dreaming Of People Who Have Died

Your person may dream of their deceased parents or siblings, friends, coworkers, or animals.

Sometimes your beloved will be able to identify clearly their experience as a dream. Other times, as your beloved moves further and further into the trajectory of dying, they may talk about having dreams that didn't seem like dreams. "It was so real," is a common comment. Your person may not be forthcoming about these experiences. It's okay to ask.

When a patient is being evaluated for hospice, you may hear the evaluator asking the patient a question about their dreams.

"Mrs. Hamilton. I wonder if you've been having any dreams of your husband or your son?"

"What was happening in the dream?"

"How did you feel about it?"

I was in the room during a hospice evaluation for a hospitalized patient. When the hospice nurse asked the question about dreams, the look on the patient's face was a combination of surprise and peace. "How did you know?" she asked.

It's so good to be affirmed, isn't it?

If your beloved is dreaming of his or her own beloveds who have died long ago, fear not. This is part of the process.

Signpost: Seeing Religious Figures

Religious figures are common visions to dying people around the world.

The figures are specific to the culture.

Christians may see Jesus or the Virgin Mary.

For Taoist in China, many believe in a deity with a human body and a cow head. In a brief conversation I had with Dr. Amy Chow, University of Hong Kong, she reports the Chinese often see Cow Head (牛头 Niútóu) as part of their dying process. Cow Head is a deity thought to escort the souls entering the Underworld.

In India, dying people may see Yama, the God of Death.

Buddhists may see the Buddha.

Not everyone sees religious figures. Many do. Some see figures of light or angels.

Here's a question your beloved might ask: "Does anyone else see that angel?"

Not Helpful:
"You're seeing things again."
"There's nothing there."

Helpful:
"What does it look like?"
"Tell them we said hello!"
"I don't see it, but I believe you."

Signpost: Seeing Or Interacting With Guides And Helpers

In the near-death experience literature, anecdotes are plentiful regarding people, clinically dead, who come back to life with stories of meeting guides, angelic entities, and helpers.

A surgeon, Dr. Mary Neal, tells about her near-death experience in her book *To Heaven and Back: A Doctor's Extraordinary Account of Her Death, Heaven, Angels, and Life Again: A True Story*.

Dr. Neal drowned in a kayaking accident. She describes being out of her body and seeing the chaos below her, and her body, from which she was now separate, under a canoe.

Her body was pulled from under the canoe and onto the shore. Once CPR was started, Dr. Neal says she went further away and guides connected with her. What intrigued me so as she recounted the story was this: with each CPR breath administered, Dr. Neal's attention was pulled back to the shore where she could see what was happening. During the 30 seconds of chest compressions between breaths, she'd go further and further away. The guides and helpers involved indicated she had work yet to do. She lived.

Just as near-death experiencers are prone to see guides or helpers, so are the dying.

These guides or helpers appear to them as people they know and people they don't. They may show up as beings of light. They may show up as angels.

The guides are there, seemingly to help with the dying person's transition from this life to wherever they're going. This idea or belief or whatever you wish to call it can be profoundly comforting to humans, especially if they're worried about their beloved dying alone.

After hearing all the stories I've heard, I'm not sure any of us really die alone.

Signpost: The Other Room

During the dying process, your person may begin to talk about another room — a room just outside in the hallway or a room upstairs when there is no upstairs.

This is one of my favorite metaphors to hear because, to me, it signals a big shift.

There are progressions in this metaphor.

For some people, first there is a conversation about 'the place'.

The 'room' or 'upstairs' or 'over there' is typically juuuust outside of where your beloved is at present. For example, they may be in a chair or bed and you'll see them motion toward a wall. They may point to and talk about 'that place over there'.

It may seem to us that your beloved's space and time are off or maybe, as I've mentioned before, just maybe *our* own space and time is off. Your beloved is functioning in a different way now. They are stepping between two worlds.

The next part in the progression of metaphor may involve conversation about 'upstairs' or 'the other room' and how they are unable to get to those places the way they wish to. Your beloved knows the other room or place is there and they may display frustration or angsty-ness because what they see, they cannot get to.

You may hear about a hallway with lots of locked doors. Keep listening. Sometime you'll hear that the doors are no longer locked and your beloved can move around freely there. That's a sign of another change.

Some of these conversations are subtle. You may hear them talk in a way that lets you know they've been there: "It was nice up there. I saw your dad."

Sometimes the dying see people in the other room, people familiar or not.

You might hear a variation of this:

"I don't know how to get into that room over there."

"There's a long hallway and I can't get in the doors."

"There's a room here that looks almost like my room at home."

"I need something off the bookshelves right there," as they motion to a blank wall.

Not Helpful:
"What are you talking about?"
"There's no room over there."
"You're seeing things."
"We had a second story in the old house, not here."

Helpful:

"I can't see the room you're talking about. Tell me what you see."

"What does the room look like, Mom?"

"How do you feel when you're up there?"

"I bet you're going to figure it out. I'll stay right here with you."

"I don't know what's happening up there either, but I bet someone will come along and help soon."

Signpost: Traveling And Trips

Your beloved may begin to talk about trains, cars, boats, or planes.

You may notice they have longed for a journey for a bit then started a process of readying themselves for it.

Now they're ready to travel.

Any kind of metaphor that allows your person to get from here to there, or allows other people whom you cannot see to get from here to there, may show up in conversation.

It's not crazy talk. I promise.

Signpost: Trains

Elizabeth was a friend of mine. She was 94 years old the last time I visited her. In the three years before this particular visit, I'd spent time with Elizabeth, learning about her life and telling her about mine. Elizabeth had a severely curved spine, difficulty walking, and after a fall had not been out of bed for a while.

On our last visit, I greeted her as I entered her room. She was tucked in her bed. A bright smile on her face, she motioned me to her for an embrace. I sat in her wheelchair beside her as we talked.

"Martha Jo! I had the most wonderful trip yesterday!" She was giddy and happy to share a tale of going to the train station. I listened, confused. She'd not been out of bed in awhile and a trip to the train station seemed a difficult proposition at best.

She continued, "I went to the train station and it was so busy! There were people everywhere! There was a big sign on the wall that kept changing. I had trouble reading it. I watched the trains come into the station. People rushed off and on. That train would leave and another would arrive."

Still confused, I asked, "Elizabeth, who was with you?"

"Well, I was by myself for awhile and I felt so lost! Then two nice young men came to help me." It was here, when she mentioned the two nice young men that

I understood.

With twinkly eyes and a wry smile she said, "They were handsome, Martha Jo. And so nice. One took my arm and the other took my suitcase. They walked me to a bench. We sat together and watched all the people. Then they brought me home."

This 'trip' to the train station, or another place where someone can be picked up or dropped off while traveling, is a common dream or vision for those who are nearing death. I say dream or vision because sometimes the dying person can differentiate between the two and sometimes not.

When Elizabeth spoke of the busy-ness of the train station and not knowing where to go, she spoke in a higher pitched voice and her face was tight. I surmised that she was a bit frightened. Once she began to talk about the young gentlemen coming to assist her, all was well. She smiled and laughed. There are often helpers in dreams and visions.

I was delighted to hear Elizabeth's story and sad when Elizabeth died a few months later. Her story was a gift.

In my TEDx talk, you'll hear me tell another story about a young boy close to death. He also left on a train.

Finally, a dying man at an inpatient hospice was agitated one afternoon. He was worried the train had come and he'd missed it. He was reassured that he'd not missed it, that it would be back for him when it was time for him to go. His family was able to meet the man where he was. He calmed. The train eventually came.

The train metaphor is a common one.

Not Helpful:
"There's no train."
"You're crazy."
"You're not making any sense."
Ignoring the comments.

Helpful:
"What an interesting story!"
"Sounds like that was a good trip for you."
"What else did you see?"

Signpost: Conversations About Cars

You may hear your beloved referencing cars. This is another common travel metaphor. As with other metaphors around traveling, caregivers often dismiss these conversations as nonsense because the person dying can't drive. Sometimes they haven't driven for years. In regular conversation, it doesn't make much sense.

In the language of dying, this is a signpost.

Is your person searching for a car, asking about their own, or suggesting they need a car to get somewhere?

Or are they talking about a car that is packed and ready to go? I have found this kind of conversation in written form or in conversations that come up soon before the person becomes mostly nonverbal. Not always! Remember, this is an individual process.

These metaphors around travel are often part of the release process. There is nothing to fear.

Signpost: Conversations About Ladders Or Ways To Get From Here To There

Butch was in his 90s. He had health problems of old age, congestive heart failure among them. He opted to go on hospice and as his dying process moved along, had visions of family members and friends.

Butch was a well-loved rugby player in South Africa as a young man. His family told me they discovered him in conversation one afternoon. Members of the rugby team had come to visit.

He noted the players had entered his room on ladders from the ceiling. He was happy to see the 'lads', as he called them, though frustrated because when they left, the lads took their ladders with them. Butch couldn't go.

Another time the lads visited, again on ladders, and left their ladders behind, but this time the ladders were too short to get Butch where he wanted to go. That time he mentioned his suitcase was packed and ready. He was frustrated they'd left again without him.

Notice how the metaphors changed. The ladders, a means to get him up and out, were not helpful in the way he needed them to be. They were taken away at first, with no chance of leaving. Then they were left for him but they were too short. And this: Butch didn't just have a suitcase, he had a *packed* suitcase.

Notice who came to visit. These were important men to him in his life.

Notice how Butch was in a liminal space, one he couldn't get out of quite yet even though some part of him felt like he was ready.

If your beloved has visitors, unseen to you, in the room, your person may or may not be able to tell you how their visitor(s) arrived or left. You can ask!

Listen for metaphors that indicate no possibility of leaving — like "the car doesn't have tires" or "the room is locked and I don't have a key" or "the ladders were taken away".

Listen for metaphors that do indicate possibility except for one thing being wrong. Phrases may be things like "too short" or "not enough" or "need more", all are common themes.

Signpost: Ready, But…

Instead of asking for a suitcase, your person may begin to talk about the suitcase being ready. It's packed.

They may talk about their car and how it's ready for the trip.

They may talk about a train that has come with family members offering greetings.

But there's something missing.

They can't find the car keys. The doors are all locked. They're waiting for a certain person to come and help them. They can see the door but can't figure out how to open it. The steps aren't down so they cannot get on the train.

Celeste's mother said, "Look!" as she motioned toward a wall. "Can you see the table?" Celeste's mama went on to describe a beautifully set table filled with food. Everything was ready, except the wine hadn't been poured. Everything is ready, but…

I watched a man fuss over his financial statements from his bed at an inpatient hospice. It took several days of visiting and revisiting those before he could feel better about whatever it was he needed to feel better about. Once he put them down, he was able to rest and died the next day.

Not Helpful:
"There's no suitcase."
"There's no car."
"You're talking crazy."
"Would you quit worrying about that stuff? It doesn't matter. I've taken care of all of it."

Helpful:
"Sounds like you're almost ready to go."
"It must be so frustrating to be ready and not have everything you need. I'm sorry, Mom. It will all be ready soon."
"When you find the keys, it'll be time to go, Dad. Have a safe trip. We love you."
"How can I help you with your papers? What do you need that you don't have?"

Signpost: Metaphors Around Releasing

When my father was so sick, there was a period of time where he fussed with the sheets on his bed and asked me to help him. With the sheets balled up in his hands, he asked for my help, "Martha, unhinge me. Unhinge me."

I put my hands over his and pressed lightly, "There you go, Papa, you're unhinged now."

He immediately calmed and his tense body relaxed. The next day we went through the same process again: "Unhinge me."

That metaphor is a doozy, isn't it? When I consider the dying process, I think about the soul and its desire to release from the body. I tell this story when I teach and often have comments about similar metaphors.

One woman told me her dying beloved said, "I just want to jump. How do I do it? How do I jump?" I asked her what she made of the comment. She believed as I that there was a push for the soul to get out somehow.

Not Helpful:
Ignoring their comments

Helpful:
Meet them where they are. If they want to be unhinged,

released, untied, the ballast cut, or some other releasing metaphor, see if you can do that in a way that will ease your beloved's need in the moment.

Signpost: Dying Person Is Grieving Too

As your beloved becomes less verbal, you may hear them cry out or sob as one would when extremely sad.

For you as a caregiver, hearing or seeing this can be tough. Our beloved is in pain. We want to fix it. We want to wrap them up in a hug and say *Don't cry*.

If you are with a patient who cries out and you aren't sure what to do, I have another invitation: Receive it. We receive laughter from people. We receive words from people. Emotion like this can be held, too. You don't need to hang onto it. It's not yours, but you can receive it.

How?

Sit there. Close your eyes if you need to. Imagine the tears are flowing as a release and your beloved is wrapped in love, whatever that looks like for you. For some, it's simply seeing their person in light. For others, imagining a religious entity holding or comforting them feels right.

I invite you, too – hold the space. By that I mean: don't make a joke. Don't change the subject. Don't turn up the television. Hold the space in which the person is releasing. These two acts of love, holding and receiving, are gorgeous gifts. Powerful ones, too.

Signpost: "Trying To Kill Me"

"You're trying to kill me." (My mother said this one to me.)
"That man/woman is trying to kill me."
"The house is falling down."
"Someone is trying to break into the house."
"The house is burning down."
"Get me out of here."

If your beloved says such things, these comments, and the behaviors that go with them, can be frightening and unsettling. The person you know isn't themselves. You try to reassure them and can't do it adequately. I've heard stories of beloveds so frightened that someone is trying to get them that they pick up something to protect themselves, not recognizing the people around them are trying to help.

You wonder if it's medication. You wonder if it's the disease process.

Here's what I want you to know:

Though every person does not display these behaviors, for those who do, these metaphors – and sometimes actions – are another part of the dying process.

These phrases and comments can happen whether or not your person is taking medication and with varying disease processes.

They can last a night or several days.

They will likely pass.

We humans are meaning-making creatures. We want to know why this is happening and what in the world to do about it.

As mentioned before, some make meaning by saying these experiences are all medication induced. Others believe it's lack of oxygen to the brain or disease process or metabolic imbalances.

Here's another way to make meaning:
Consider the possibility that the ego and body are all wrapped up together, and the spirit is separate.
The ego is *extraordinarily* attached to the body. The body is about to not need the ego anymore, so it's freaking out!

For you — the caregiver, child, parent, sibling, or spouse — instead of taking the comments above at face value, think of them as a metaphor.

The house is the body:
"The body is burning down."
"The body is falling down."
"You're trying to kill my body."
"Get me out of here so I'll be safe."

This is the ego's last ditch effort to hang on to all it's known. It's a tough process to watch, exhausting for the dying person and exhausting in a different way for those watching it all unfold.

Then...blessedly, there is rest. Not death, but stillness.

Whatever the fight was has ceased.

You may experience your person here, in the hospital bed before you, with their eyes searching a faraway place.

There is free-flowing movement between the body and spirit now, where the spirit of your person is in and out, in and out, in and out, then finally out.

What can you do to help during this time?

Reassure your person they are safe.

Ask your hospice team if medication to calm your person is appropriate.

Don't take the comments personally.

Remember this is part of the trajectory of dying and likely won't last a long time.

Movements

One part of the trajectory of the dying process involves movement. As the dying process moves along, the kinds of movement change. You may see people pick at things on themselves or on a blanket that they can see and others can't.

Another kind of movement is reaching out toward people they see that others cannot. And as the process moves along, the reaching changes from the action kind, where they were in the space and time of some other place, to being in the room and reaching toward other people or entities (or whatever you want to call them) who are also in the room.

Eventually, the reaching becomes very pronounced and upward so they are reaching up to the sky, and they may have a grimace on their face as though they can't quite get to the thing they want to get to.

There is another kind of movement related to previous experiences the dying had in life. I'll talk about that next.

Signpost: Back In Time

Your dying person may begin to move her hands as though she's picking up something off the bed no one else can see.

She may reach toward things or move things again, things not visible to anyone else but her.

Watch closely. You may see your person acting out a situation from earlier in their life.

Some near-death experiencers have a life review. They go back to previous times in their lives and see it all happening.

The dying have life reviews, too, except they're not watching it. They're in it. For dying people, they aren't watching their life, they are back in a part of it. Anne's dad shot skeet from his hospital bed. I watched a man seemingly bridle a horse. My aunt spoke of walking around a city she lived in 40 years before. They go back there and are in it for a time.

I've watched dying people sew, open books, cook, eat. I watched my father, a retired minister, put on his stole as he prepared himself for a Sunday service.

These motions are often dismissed, again as nonsense. This is part of the sorting and sifting process. They're making sense of where they've been. They're releasing and preparing to move on to the next place.

Hospital and hospice staff don't know your beloved as you do. They may see arms moving around and not think another thing about it. You, because you know your person so well, may be able to notice that your beloved is doing something from their life from before. Butch, the gentleman I mentioned in the story about the ladders, worked in the mines in South Africa. One afternoon he held out his hand and said he had some machine parts he wanted to make sure didn't get lost.

His daughter met him where he was. She fetched a Ziploc and held it out for her dad to put the machine parts, that only he could see, into the bag. He was calmer and able to rest after that.

Meet your person where they are. I cannot say that enough.

Signpost: Reaching

Your beloved may move their hands and arms as part of the dying process.

The movements may be subtle: a finger moving, then the hand. There can be full body twitches that happen near the end of life, like ones you may sometimes have as you're falling asleep.

And there is reaching.

There's a difference in the movements that happen with the life review like we talked about in the previous pages, and the reaching we'll talk about now.

The life review movements correspond to something the person did at some previous time in their lives, like my dad putting on his vestments for a church service.

Reaching is different. It is present time. The dying person is connecting to some unseen something and reaching toward or for it.

At first the movements are around them. If your beloved is lying on their back, they may raise their hand up, as though motioning to someone.

The reaching can go to the sides, too, as though they're reaching over to someone on their left or their right.

They may reach toward the end of the bed.

Later they may begin reaching upwards, a bit higher than before.

While this is happening, they may or may not have their eyes open.

If their eyes are open, their gaze often changes along with the movements — looking and reaching around the bed, then midway around the room, then often to the top of the room.

You may see your beloved reaching as high as they can, up toward the ceiling directly above them. They may have a grimace on their face as though they're frustrated or mightily determined to connect with something unseen to the rest of us. Try as they will, they can't quite get to the thing they want to get to.

Not Helpful:
Putting your hand on theirs to stop them from reaching.

Helpful:
You can notice aloud what you see: "You are reaching for something, William. I see you."
You can notice, not say anything, and hold space.
If the reaching is the high overhead kind, you can say, "You're almost ready to go, aren't you, Max? Go with them whenever you want to. We'll be fine here."

Caveat: Another reminder – these behaviors aren't predictors.

Signpost: Shared Death Experience

"The Shared Death Experience (SDE) [is] a profound experience whereby a loved one, caregiver or bystander shares a dying person's *initial* transition from this world into the afterlife."
from www.SharedCrossing.com

In other words, the dying person and the person(s) who are tending them share a similar experience where both see, hear, or feel the same experience as the dying person is transitioning from this life.

William Peters is the founder of the Shared Crossing Training Program and SharedCrossing.com. In 2014, the Shared Crossing Training Program, designed to facilitate the SDE, was a central component of a $250,000 research study conducted by researchers from the Religion, Experience, and Mind Lab Group at University of California, Santa Barbara. This is cutting-edge research on a fascinating aspect related to how we humans experience dying. Data collected so far shows about 40% of participants have experienced the SDE.

Dr. Raymond Moody, the author of the seminal book on near-death experiences, says 10% of his audiences answer *yes* when he asks if anyone has had a Shared Death Experience.

I mention Dr. Moody because the core experiences of a Shared Death Experience are similar to many of the elements in the Near-Death Experience. Also from

SharedCrossing.com, some examples of elements that have been experienced by those having an SDE:

- Mist at Death
- Hearing Beautiful Music
- Change in the Geometry of the Room
- Strong Upward Pull on the Body
- Shared Out-of-Body Experience
- Seeing a Mystical Light
- Empathically Co-living the Life Review of the Dying Person
- Greeted by Beings of Light
- Encountering Heavenly Realms
- Boundary in the Heavenly Realm

Just like the dying process is never the same from one person to another, no SDEs are exactly the same. There *are* common elements and experiencers of SDEs report profound benefits.

I have not experienced an SDE though I have talked with a number of people who have. In each instance, the person has shared how calming, peaceful, and helpful the experience was for them.

If you have experienced an SDE and would like to learn more or share what happened to you, I encourage you to go to the Shared Crossing website www.SharedCrossing.com.

Signpost: Rallying

Your person will become quieter, sleeping more and more. They may be agitated by moments, then able to rest. You may awaken one morning and your person is as clear and present as they can be. They can talk to you or respond. They may ask for something to eat.

It's a hopeful time for many, as it seems the dying person is improving.

This uptick in activity and clear cognition is part of the trajectory of dying for many.

It's difficult to say if a rally is a rally until it's over and your person doesn't rouse again. Is this a rally? Is it not? Are they going to get better? All valid questions. If your person is on hospice, they are likely not going to have a remarkable turnaround. I surely have known patients who've gone off hospice service and lived awhile longer. Those situations are few and far between.

What can you do during what might be a rally? What you'd do any other time your person is awake and alert.

Be present as best you can be.

Put your phone away and really be in the moment.

Hold their hand.

Tell them a story.

Ask them to tell you a story.

Find something to laugh about together.

Be silent together.

Listen to music together.

If there's anything you need to say, say it.

Thoughts On Pain Medicine

There are people who choose not to have pain medicine as part of their dying process.

Some don't want to miss out on any moments with their families. They worry pain medication will impair them. They want to die consciously.

Some are frightened they'll get addicted.

Some are fearful of the way the medicine will make them feel.

A woman I was with this year had a tumor taken from her jaw. The scar went all the way up and under her right ear. She'd been at hospice for a day. She'd refused pain medication.

As I sat with her, she moved her hand back and forth, back and forth over the scar and moaned softly. The space between her eyes was tight. Her face was red.

I leaned in. I looked her in the eye and spoke softly.

"Ms. H., I'm seeing you, how you're squinting your eyes. How your face is a bit red. How you're rubbing your jaw. Ms. H., the staff can give you medicine to take the edge off so you won't hurt so much."

She kept looking at me. No movement except to rub her jaw.

I continued, "Ms. H., the medicine won't make you die. The medicine helps people relax and hopefully eases the pain. There are times that people get so relaxed they let go, but they don't do that until they're ready. You look like you're in a lot of pain. Can I ask the staff to get you some medicine?"

Ever so slightly, Ms. H. nodded her head yes. I nodded back and squeezed her hand.

She couldn't swallow any longer so the medicine was administered through a mask. I put on my own mask so as not to take in any of her medication. Once it was done, I took off her mask and held her hand. She pulled my hand to her face. Squeezed gently. It was her way to say *Thank you.*

I talked to another gentleman similarly about pain medication. He refused. I tried again. He refused. I wanted him to be more comfortable. He had his own agenda and his agenda had nothing to do with me. I asked twice. He refused twice. I got the message. My need for him to be more comfortable was MY need, not his.

Consider what your beloved needs and if your needs are helpful or getting in the way. We don't mean for the latter to happen, but it sure can. Just notice. That's all.

Signpost: Body Changes

A number of physical changes will happen as your beloved is nearing death. Some things you may notice:

Their skin will likely get thin, paper thin in some cases. It will look translucent.

Fingernails will often turn a bluish tint.

Your beloved's ears may 'pin'. This means rather than their ears being away from the head as they had been, the pressure of the pillow will cause their ears to stay against their head. Some don't notice this at all. Some do and get concerned. This is common and I want you to know about it in case you see it. You're most likely to notice this when your beloved is moved from side to side to change their position.

There will be a time when it's likely difficult for your person to keep their mouth closed.

Their lips will turn in a bit against their teeth. They'll breathe through their mouth.

Their temperature will rise and fall. Your person may sweat then shiver.

You will likely notice muscle tone waning and arms and legs losing bulk.

You may notice mottling or blotches of purplish or

bluish colors on the backs of legs, feet, backs of arms. This means the blood isn't circulating and instead is pooling.

Your person may have difficulty closing their eyes or one eye may be open and another closed.

These are all signposts of change in the trajectory of dying.

Signpost: Breathing

Breathing changes over the course of the dying process. There will be times when your person sounds as though they are snoring.

There will be a time when they have difficulty keeping their mouth closed and the snoring/breathing may be louder still.

There will be times when the space between breaths becomes pronounced. You may be able to count 15-30 seconds or more between breaths. This can begin to happen several days before a person dies. It is a little unnerving when you first notice. You may notice yourself not breathing as you wait for them to take a breath.

More changes in breathing occur in the final days and final hours. For some this is subtle, for others these changes are substantial. Often agitation will decrease and changes in breathing will be more noticeable.

As your beloved moves into their final hours, the sound of their breathing may be akin to a loud snore, though you will likely hear along with it a rattly sound. You may hear this referred to as *agonal breathing* or *the death rattle*. This type of breathing can go on, with spaces in between, for a few hours or many hours.

If you don't know what to expect or haven't heard the

agonal breathing sounds before, they can be frightening. Please remember, the dying are between two worlds. What we see happening here is not the whole story. The suffering we believe is happening may not be.

You can help by focusing on your own breath and calming yourself. That energy will translate to your beloved as they are working to let go.

Signpost: Fevers

Your beloved will have a fever as part of their dying process.

When someone is dying, the thermostat in their body goes on the fritz. Hot. Cold. Hot. Cold.

There are times when your beloved will be feverish and sweating. There will be times when they want to be covered because they're cold. There will be other times when their extremities are cooler and their core is warm. These cycles will happen over the course of your beloved's dying process.

If you have questions about this part of the dying experience, ask your hospice professional. Someone is on call 24 hours a day, 7 days a week. If you wake up at 2 am and have a question, call them. That's why they're there.

A client of mine mentioned the difficulty the nursing home staff were having rolling her father to give him a suppository. She indicated this was a difficult process for all involved, especially her father who was in pain when moved. Said I, "Why is he getting suppositories?" "For his fevers," she replied.

I encouraged my client to speak to her dad's hospice nurse. I invited her to share that the nursing home staff members were medicating her dad for fevers. I encouraged her to ask if this was necessary. (The hospice colleagues I'm in contact with are staunch supporters of comfort care and I had a hunch something was off here.)

Indeed, the hospice nurse didn't know about the suppositories. The staff at the nursing home were following their own protocols, doing what they do when a nursing home patient has a fever. They weren't doing anything wrong. However, my client's dad wasn't a nursing home patient any longer. He was a hospice patient.

Some patients and families may want fevers medicated. Some may not. You get to decide.

If something is happening with your beloved's care that seems to be more agitating or hurtful than helpful, ask if it's necessary.

Leaving When They're Ready

We die in our own ways on our own terms. For example, some die with family and friends beside us. We wait until the last person arrives — to hear them, to feel their energy in the room, to say good-bye and then let go.

In contrast, some who are dying wait until visitors, family, and friends have left the room, maybe for a new cup of coffee or a quick trip home for a nap. In the quiet moments, they go.

I've talked with agitated family members who have encouraged and given permission to the dying to go, and still they stay. The permission-giving is important for both the receiver and the giver. Once it's done, the dying will make their next move when they're good and ready.

My hunch, the dying have power over when they take their leave. Or maybe the energy shifts in the room just enough that they can let go. I don't understand how it works though I've seen it demonstrated over and over again.

Many people I talk with are burdened because they feel as though they missed their beloved's last breath.

"Martha, I just stepped out for a moment."

"I can't believe he died while I was out of the room."

"I wanted to be with her. I shouldn't have left."

If this happens for you, please know you didn't make a mistake. I believe your person needed to leave the way they did.

What To Do:
As your beloved moves closer to death, they engage with the world around them less and less. It will be difficult for them to open their eyes or speak. They may no longer squeeze your finger or answer questions.

For as long as I can remember, I've heard people talk about how dying people can still hear us, that hearing is the last to go.

They can feel us, too. They know we're in the room.

A nurse friend of mine told of an ICU patient who was near death. The large extended family piled in the room around the bed. There was much weeping and conversation. The nurse had a sense that her patient needed calm to be able to die. She asked the family to leave, except for the patient's two daughters. Within minutes, the patient died.

Think about how your person was in regular life. An introvert? Loved to be around people? Needed their quiet time? Liked to be alone reading books in the corner? Didn't like for people to make a fuss over them? Loved a party?

That might give you some clues.

Another thing to do? Ask them, before they get to the place where they can't talk to you, if they'd like to be alone or not when they take their last breath. Tell them, too, what you'd like. "Mom, I'd like to be with you when it's time and I understand if you need to do something different."

Meaning-Making

You and I are meaning-making creatures. We seek to find reasons for things that happen in our lives.

When someone we love is dying, we look for meaning to attribute to what's happening.

When our beloved begins to see and hear things no one else in the room can see or hear, some who witness these events will assume the behaviors are related to pain medication or disease process.

Others will be certain that the visions, sounds, or behaviors of the dying are part of a grander spiritual adventure with the deathbed experiences indicating life beyond this life.

The Signposts of Dying happen to humans all around the world.

The meaning you make of them is your own — and the meaning your beloved makes of them is theirs.

I've said it a bunch of times already, and I'll say it once more for good measure: regardless of the meaning you make of the signposts of dying, please meet your beloved right where they are.

Accept their experience as real for them.

Acknowledge your own feelings with someone you

trust.

Laugh when you need to laugh.

Tears are good. No need to hold them back.

When you decide you can be someone who helps walk another out of this world, you've engaged in a tender, precious kind of love.

You can do this.

Now What?

My hope for this book: Start a conversation that travels far and wide about what happens when someone is dying. As my smart friend Laurie Foley says, "People really don't know how to talk about this at all." This book and others like it could be a start.

I invite you to send a copy to someone you know who is walking a beloved out of this world. Your note can say something like this: "*Signposts of Dying* helped me understand the dying process in a different way. Maybe it can help you, too."

Invite a group of friends or family to read the book then host a dinner party.

Host a Google Hangout or Skype gathering where you talk about what you want to have happen at the end of your life or what your experiences have been as you've companioned dying people.

Here are some conversation starters:

"What is the first death you remember?"

"What was the first death that you felt deeply?"

"Have you ever been with a dying person? What do you recall about that experience?"

"What do you think happens after we die? What got

87

you to that belief?"

"When you think about dying people seeing loved ones who died long ago, what meaning do you make of those experiences?"

"Have you been with anyone who engaged in some of the signposts explained in this book? Did you recognize them at the time? Do you recognize them now after reading?"

"What's changed for you as a result of reading this book?"

"What have you thought about concerning the end of your life? Have you shared your thoughts with anyone? Could you? Would you?"

You've got your own questions, too, I imagine. Ask them in your inner circles with people you trust.

Finally, I invite you to tell your dying stories, the ones you have from being at the bedside of a dying person. Talk about the visions and the movements. Talk about how the language didn't make sense sometimes, along with the times that it did. Talk about your fears and the coincidences, the struggles and the relief.

Storytelling around these topics is a special kind of honoring, I think. An honoring of ourselves, our experiences and the experiences of our beloveds. If you have questions, comments or stories about *Signposts of*

Dying, email me: signposts@marthaatkins.com.

Resources

Here are a few more resources about dying that may be helpful. I've only included a few so as not to overwhelm.

- Martha Jo Atkins' Website – www.MarthaAtkins.com

- Martha Jo Atkins Death and Dying Institute – martha-jo-atkins.mykajabi.com

- End of Life University – www.eoluniversity.com

- Shared Crossing Project about Shared Death Experiences – www.SharedCrossing.com

- Final Words Project – www.FinalWordsProject.org
  A few months after my father recovered from his illness in 2014, I met linguist Lisa Smartt and Dr. Raymond Moody. Dr. Moody is best known for his work on Near Death Experiences (NDEs) and his book *Life After Life*. Dr. Moody shared that for most of his career, in addition to NDE research, he's been interested in and categorizing the unintelligible words of the dying.

  Lisa Smartt is doing her own work to further our understanding of the language of the dying. As the founder of the Final Words Project, Lisa is working with Dr. Moody and Dr. Erica Goldblatt Hyatt to record the final words of the dying in real-time. This is research that's never been done before in this way.

The project begins January 2016, conducted through Bryn Athyn College. I mention these colleagues because you need to know who they are and keep an eye out for what their research reveals.

- Dying Matters – dyingmatters.org

- *Being Mortal: Medicine and What Matters in the End*, (2014) Atul Gawande

- *Final Gifts*, (2012) Maggie Callanan and Patricia Kelley

- *To Heaven and Back: A Doctor's Extraordinary Account of Her Death, Heaven, Angels, and Life Again: A True Story*, (2012) Dr. Mary Neal

Thank You

Thank you for reading this guidebook. If it's been helpful, please go online and leave a review www.marthaatkins.com/SODreview. More reviews mean more people are likely to see this book and find help about a topic that causes angst and confusion for so many.

As difficult as it can be to walk someone you love out of this world, the experience can be one of the most meaningful and profound of your life.

I wish that for you.

Acknowledgments

Deep Love and Thanks To:

Heather Trepal, dissertation chair extraordinaire.

Michele Woodward and Laurie Foley for their friendship and stellar advice.

Crys Wood for elegant help getting this out to the world.

Erin Tyler for gorgeous book graphics.

Betsy and Pam for that delicious writing retreat in Sedona, FFS.

Patti Digh for teaching me about strong offers.

Fabeku for helping me step into better versions of myself.

Jo Pillmore for stellar mindset work that led us into a fine friendship.

Lydia, Jan, Liz, Kelli, and Sheri encouragers one and all.

Rachel for getting me organized, keeping me moving, and being the best kind of friend.

Gloria and her family for allowing me to be a part of such a beautiful ending.

Beloveds who've shared their stories, I'm so grateful.

Suzette for believing in the possibilities and sharing life with me.

John and Dad, deep love and thanks for your encouragement.

Jim – I miss you.

Belle, Gam, Mom, Aunt Betty, Aunt Margaret, I'm proud to be in your lineage.